Y0-DKC-569

Y BIO
MAP

DATE DUE

NOV 23 2003

NOV 1 5 2004

JAN 1 7 2007

P

1. Bo
be renew
7 day bo

2. A fi
on each
to the ab
any pers
been paid

3. All
wear and
satisfactio

4. Eac
books dra
cruing on

34314

JAMES MADISON

About the Book

James Madison was called Jemmy when he was a young-
ster. Always small and usually ill, he was seldom robust
enough to attend school. He studied at home until he
was twelve, and after that he became strong enough to
go off to school. Later, still small, but much healthier,
James Madison served his country as an expert on law,
as a delegate from Virginia to the Continental Congress,
and as President of the United States.

E PLURIBUS UNUM

A See and Read
Beginning to Read Biography

JAMES MADISON

by Patricia Miles Martin

Illustrated by Richard Cuffari

G. P. Putnam's Sons
New York

To my uncle, James Marion White

JAMES MADISON

Ten-year-old Jemmy, as James Madison
was called, sat high in an old oak tree in
the forest. He sat so still that a squirrel came
creeping along the branch toward him.

Jemmy didn't move, and the squirrel
sat up and looked at him.

Jemmy knew that when he sat quietly,
he learned about the little animals in
the forest–squirrels and rabbits, catbirds
and owls.

Not far from the forest was the big house on the plantation where Jemmy lived. Around the house were tiny cabins for slaves, barns for horses and cows, and sheds for sheep.

Jemmy had been born in 1751. He was
born in the Colony of Virginia. That was a
time when the Thirteen American Colonies
belonged to England. And the English and
the French were fighting each other for land
in America. Indians helped the French
in the fighting.

9

Jemmy could remember a time when he was four years old. Not far from his home, the English had lost a battle to the French and Indians.

Everyone on the plantation knew that the Indians might come upon them at any hour. At any hour, they might hear the war cry of the Indians.

Everyone was filled with terror, and men
kept watch through the night.

The Indians did not come to the
plantation, but Jemmy would never forget
that time, long ago.

In his ten years, Jemmy learned many things.

He knew that the Indians were still fighting far to the north, and the people on the plantation were not afraid.

Jemmy's father had moved his family to their new house on a wooded hill. It would be called Montpelier. It was a big house that would hold a big family.

Jemmy climbed down from the oak tree
and made his way through the forest.

The plantation where he lived was like
a small village.

Slaves cut down trees to make cabins
and sheds. They cut wood to burn in the
great fireplaces inside the house. They
worked in the fields.

15

Because Jemmy was small and often sick, he studied at home. He did not go to school until he was almost twelve years old. But he knew more than many of the boys in school. And later, Jemmy and the younger children in his family studied with a teacher at home.

The French and Indian War was over, but there was still trouble in the Colonies.

Jemmy and his teacher talked about these troubles. They talked about the laws that England made to govern the Colonies. Jemmy knew that the Colonies wanted to make their own laws.

A few years went by, and Jemmy was ready to go away to college in the tiny village of Princeton.

Jemmy's father did not want him to go alone on a long trip, so two friends and a slave rode with him.

They rode horseback along a muddy path that led through the forest.

Jemmy listened to the call of the catbirds in the green trees and to the slurp of the horses' hooves in the red-brown mud.

At college, three boys lived in each room,
and they studied until late, by candlelight.

Jemmy learned all that he could learn about the governments of other countries. He learned quickly in all his studies but one. He had trouble learning to speak in public.

Later, when he had to stand and speak in a room filled with men, he would remember what the president of the college had said:

"Never do you speak unless you have something to say, and when you are done, be sure to leave off."

After the boys studied at night, they talked and laughed together.

When the sleepy president of the college heard them, he called out, "To bed, lads, to bed!" Then they waited quietly until he had gone away, and they talked again, far into the night.

After college, James Madison went back to the plantation and taught his own brothers and sisters.

With books piled high beside him, he still found time to read and study.

England had made new laws, and the Colonies did not want to obey them. And because of this, England sent soldiers to the Colonies to make them obey the English laws.

Many men picked up their rifles, ready
to meet the English soldiers.

James Madison was with the men who
were ready to fight, but he was too small
and sickly to be a soldier.

American and English soldiers met, and
shots were fired.

This was a new war–the Revolutionary
War.

Young James Madison was asked to go
to Williamsburg to help make new laws
for Virginia.

He was still afraid to speak in public,
but he talked to a few men at a time. The
men listened. And as they listened, they
knew that small James Madison knew
more about governments than most of the
other men who were there to make the laws.

The constitution of Virginia was written
–laws that would govern the State of
Virginia. No longer would Virginia obey
English laws.

James Madison made many new friends
at Williamsburg, and one of these was
Thomas Jefferson.

Very soon after this time, the lawmakers
in Philadelphia declared that the Thirteen
Colonies were free states, with the right to
make their own laws.

Laws were quickly written to govern the
new states.

James Madison went to the Congress
at Philadelphia, as a delegate from the State
of Virginia.

When the Revolutionary War was over, many American soldiers had not been given pay for the time they were in the Army. Soldiers marched to Philadelphia and waited outside the building where the Congress was meeting. They wanted their money.

But Congress had no money. And Congress did not have the right to get money from the new states. James Madison knew that new laws were needed to govern the states. There should be new laws for the good of all people.

Time passed, and the thirteen states did not work together. Some of the states wanted to make their own laws. Many states were not friendly to one another. Sometimes one state would not let another state use its river, yet they all needed to use the rivers. They needed to do many things together.

After three years in Congress, James Madison went back to Montpelier to study law. And his good friend Thomas Jefferson sent books to help him with this study.

The new states were asked to send
delegates to the Congress in Philadelphia.
The delegates would write the new laws
that were needed if the states were to
work together.

James Madison was the delegate from
Virginia.

Through forests and past farms, he
rode away to Philadelphia.

He waited in Philadelphia for the delegates to come from other states–those men who would help make the new laws.

At last the delegates came from five states.

But five were not enough.

Nothing could be done until delegates came from seven of the thirteen states.

James Madison wondered if they would come. He wondered if the states would ever be united for the good of all the states.

Without laws to govern all of them, each state would be like a small country.

There would be no United States.

At last, the delegates came.

Small James Madison played a great part
in the making of the Constitution. Every
day he was in the Congress, talking . . .
talking . . .

It seemed that men would never agree.
It seemed that the delegates from the big

states would never agree with those from
the little states. But James Madison did not
stop trying to make every delegate see
how great was the need for new laws.

And little by little, law by law, the
Constitution was written.

But there was still trouble to come.

Of the thirteen states, nine states would have to sign this Constitution before it would become law.

James Madison and two other men reached the people through newspapers.

They told people why the states should work together. They told people why their states should sign the Constitution.

At last, nine states signed, and there was a new government in the United States.

Three more states signed. But Rhode Island, the littlest state of all, would not sign.

There was a first President of the United States, George Washington. And James Madison was a Representative from Virginia in the first Congress.

Now, James Madison was not afraid to speak in public. In Congress, he talked about the rights of all people. Ten new laws, setting forth these rights, were made a part of the Constitution. These ten laws were called the Bill of Rights.

At last, the state of Rhode Island signed the Constitution, and thirteen states were united–the United States of America.

The second Congress met in Philadelphia. While James Madison was there, he met Dolley Todd. Mrs. Todd had one small boy. Soon Mr. Madison and Mrs. Todd were married.

Two years later Mr. Madison took his family back to Montpelier to live.

A second President was chosen by the people. And four years later Thomas Jefferson became the third President of the United States. He chose Mr. Madison to be his Secretary of State. Mr. Madison and his family went to the little city of Washington to live.

The United States had to face new
trouble.

Pirates were capturing American ships.

And over the sea, the English and the
French were at war again.

On the sea, England stopped American
ships and took American men to fight
with the English Navy.

English ships waited in American waters
and captured American ships.

Then James Madison was chosen to be
the fourth President of the United States.

He asked Congress to declare war against
England, and this was done.

The United States was at war.

The war with England went on and on.

English soldiers came to the United States. Not far from Washington, they saw American soldiers coming along the road to meet them.

And President Madison was riding with the soldiers.

A soldier asked the President to leave before the men met in battle.

The English soldiers marched into
Washington. Buildings were burned. The
English moved on, leaving a burning city.
Great rains came, and the fires were
put out, and the city was safe.

When the battles were over and the war was ended, President Madison asked Congress for an Army and a Navy to protect the United States, and the Congress agreed.

James Madison was President of the United States for eight years. After that time, he went again to Montpelier. He and Mrs. Madison lived on his great old plantation, with its sheds for sheep, barns for horses and cows, and tiny cabins for slaves.

James Madison always said that he did not believe that it was right to make men slaves. But he would not live to see the day when slaves would be set free.

When Mr. Madison was eighty-five years old, he died at Montpelier.

James Madison worked for his state and for his country almost all his long life.

Then people spoke of him as "the great little Madison."

Now he is remembered as the Father of the Constitution.

Key Words

agree
Army
battle
born
cabins
captured, capturing
college
Colony, Colonies
Congress
Constitution
declared
delegate
died
Dolley Todd
eighty-five
England
English
fourth
free
French
George Washington
govern
governments
hooves
James Madison
Jemmy
lads
laws
life
marched
married
Montpelier

Navy
obey
Philadelphia
pirates
plantation
President
Princeton
public
Representative
Revolutionary
Rhode Island
rifles
secretary
sheds
sign
slaves
slurp
soldiers
speak
state
study, studied
sure
taught
thirteen
Thomas Jefferson
united
unless
Virginia
war
Williamsburg
written

63

The Author

PATRCIA MILES MARTIN is a biographer and story-teller and has written *See and Read* biographies of six Presidents, including Jefferson Davis of the Confederacy. The other five are John Fitzgerald Kennedy, Zachary Taylor, Abraham Lincoln, James Madison, and Andrew Jackson.

Mrs. Martin, born in Cherokee, Kansas, grew up on the prairie lands of eastern Colorado, and now lives in San Mateo, California. Her other biographies include *Jacqueline Kennedy Onassis, Pocahontas, John Marshall,* and *Dolley Madison.*